THE LAST DAYS OF STEAM IN

KENT

THE LAST DAYS OF STEAM IN

KENT

-MARTIN R. GALLEY-

ALAN SUTTON

First published in the United Kingdom in 1991 by
Alan Sutton Publishing Ltd · Phoenix Mill · Far Thrupp · Stroud · Gloucestershire

First published in the United States of America in 1991 by
Alan Sutton Publishing Inc. · Wolfeboro Falls · NH 03896–0848

British Library Cataloguing in Publication Data

Galley, Martin
The last days of steam in Kent.
1. Kent. Railway services: British Rail. Southern Region. Steam
I. Title
625.261094223

ISBN 0-86299-887-5

Library of Congress Cataloging in Publication Data applied for

Endpapers: Front: E1 class 4–4–0 No. 31497 nears the top of Herne Bay bank with a Kent coast excursion train on 10.8.58.

Back: E1 class 4–4–0 No. 31497 heads a westbound Sunday morning vans train towards Teynham on 17.8.58

Front Cover: H class 0–4–4T No. 31533 on the Westerham branch train between Brasted and Chevening on 15.4.61.

Back Cover: N class 2–6–0 No. 31414 pulls away from Faversham station with an engineer's train on 22.9.58.

Typeset in Palatino 9/10.
Typesetting and origination by
Alan Sutton Publishing Limited.
Printed in Great Britain by
The Bath Press, Avon.

Introduction

The author spent his youth living within sight and sound of the ex-LC&DR main line at Beckenham Junction, attended school near Kent House station and spent many hours watching the Kent coast expresses and boat trains that ran between the numerous inner and outer suburban electric trains. Summer Saturday evenings provided special entertainment with the returning holiday extras and the bonus of a C class 0-6-0 shunting the goods yard at Beckenham Junction. On rare occasions, one of the extras would take the spur onto the Mid-Kent line at New Beckenham. Once involved with railway photography, excursions were made further afield to the junctions near Chislehurst and beyond to the challenging gradients near Sole Street. A few years prior to the end of steam in Kent the author had moved to Whitstable and was able to continue photographing steam at the other end of the county.

Although many of the outer suburban lines had been electrified just prior to the Second World War, the ex-SE&CR main line services to Thanet and the Channel ports remained steam operated into the 1950s. Even some branch lines close to London, such as those to Gravesend West, Westerham and Allhallows-on-Sea, had escaped electrification and were still outposts of steam operation in among the third rails.

There was a great variety of steam locomotives to be seen in Kent: almost all surviving ex-SE&CR types plus those of SR origin ranging from Bulleid's 'Merchant Navy' class on the boat trains to an ex-LB&SCR A1X at Rolvenden. The Kent coast lines were particularly noted for the large number of 4-4-0s that were still used on express passenger services. In addition to the 'Schools', these included classes D1, E1, L and L1, but the more elegant E and D classes had mostly departed by the 1950s to spend their last days on other parts of the Southern Region. Kent coast expresses were usually the preserve of Bulleid 'Light Pacifics', 'King Arthur' and 'Schools' classes but secondary and freight services brought 'moguls' and 0-6-0s. Foreigners included LMS style 2-6-4Ts and 2-6-2Ts on east Kent secondary services, 'Black 5' 4-6-0s on excursions and, at the end, GWR pannier tanks on the Folkestone harbour branch.

After 1951 the BR standard classes began to appear with two 'Britannias', Nos. 70004 and 70014, being assigned to the boat trains and then later, standard class 5 4-6-0s became commonplace on the Kent coast expresses. Ex-LNER types were not usually seen but several B1 class 4-6-0s appeared in April and May 1953 when all the Bulleid 'Pacifics' were temporarily withdrawn for inspection after one of their number had suffered a driving axle failure at Crewkerne on 24 April 1953.

After the war, the status quo remained until the advent of the Modernization Plan of 1955 when plans were published for the progressive elimination of steam from Kent by the early 1960s. The first steam service to disappear was the Charing Cross to Hastings service in 1957 when the ageing narrow-bodied stock, mostly hauled by 'Schools' class locomotives, was replaced by diesel electric multiple units. This service terminated in Sussex but the first 34 miles to Tunbridge Wells passed through Kent.

Main line steam services through Kent were mostly regular interval services, augmented by extra services to the City in rush hours and interspersed with boat-train workings to the channel ports. On summer weekends and bank holidays, there was an extraordinary increase in the frequency of trains to popular seaside destinations around the Kent coast, particularly to Thanet. These summer excursion trains were a railway photographer's delight because they left London in a steady stream from early morning and, travelling eastwards, would be well lit on a sunny day. In the evening, when the sun had conveniently moved round, the westward procession back to London began. At the peak of the season, anything that moved was pressed into service and it was not unusual to see class C, Q and Q1 0–6–0s taking trains all the way to Ramsgate.

The north Kent coast, Thanet and Dover were served by the ex-LC&DR main line from Victoria via Herne Hill or the Catford loop to Bromley South. As the preferred route was via Herne Hill, it is not surprising that the Catford loop was seldom frequented by steam photographers. The passenger service on the steam operated branch from Longfield to Gravesend West survived until August 1953 and was usually operated by an H class 0–4–4T from Farningham Road. Outer suburban electric services ended at Gillingham and the main line trains went on to serve Sittingbourne, Faversham and then most stations to Margate and Ramsgate. The intermediate stations at Rainham and Newington were served by local trains and by some of the services to Sheerness-on-Sea. In steam days there were only a few through trains from Victoria to Canterbury East and Dover via the LC&DR main line, passengers having to change to stopping trains at Faversham.

Main line interval services to Folkestone and Dover ran non-stop from Charing Cross over the ex-SER route through Hither Green, Orpington to Sevenoaks and Tonbridge. At Dunton Green, on the London side of Sevenoaks, the steam-operated branch to Westerham diverged from the electrified main line. The Charing Cross to Hastings services also used this route as far as Tonbridge before climbing away through High Brooms to Tunbridge Wells. Eastward from Tonbridge the SER mainline passed through Paddock Wood where steam operated branches ran to Hawkhurst and Maidstone West. At Headcorn, until January 1954, K&ESR trains to Tenterden still left from the bay platform. Beyond Ashford at Sandling Junction was the branch line to Hythe but the passenger service had gone by 1952. Main line trains to Folkestone and Dover usually continued around the coast via Deal to Ramsgate.

Boat-train services started from Victoria but used a variety of routes to reach Folkestone and Dover, depending on the time of day and congestion from other traffic. The Folkestone services used the LC&DR route to Bickley Junction and then down the SER main line through Tonbridge and Ashford. At Folkestone Junction reversal was necessary for the short journey on the heavily graded branch to Folkestone harbour. Dover services could use this route too but also ran all the way on the LC&DR main line via Faversham. The Otford–Maidstone–Ashford line was used as a relief route for both services. Peak hour long distance commuter services were run to and from Cannon Street and those serving Thanet were routed over the otherwise freight only spur lines connecting St Mary Cray Junction with Chislehurst Junction.

In the early 1950s, steam operated secondary routes within or penetrating Kent, included Maidstone East to Ashford; Ramsgate to Ashford via Minster and Canterbury West; Ashford to Hastings via Appledore and Rye, including the New Romney branch; Tunbridge Wells West into Sussex and Tonbridge to Redhill.

All freight traffic was of course steam-hauled and tended to be concentrated where possible on the ex-SER routes rather than along the more steeply graded ex-LC&DR lines through the Medway towns.

Steam depots in Kent were located at Hither Green, Gillingham, Faversham, Ramsgate, Dover, Folkestone, Ashford, Tonbridge and Tunbridge Wells West. The Works at Ashford continued to handle steam engines until about 1960.

There was a lot of industrial steam in Kent, mostly associated with the cement works, paper mills and collieries. Narrow gauge steam systems that survived the war included the Chattenden and Upnor Naval Tramway, the extensive Bowaters system at Sittingbourne and the Romney, Hythe and Dymchurch Railway.

Photographing steam trains in Kent was made easier by the varied terrain, sharp gradients and the general east–west orientation of the main routes. One could always be sure of getting good smoke effects at locations such as Sole Street bank, on the climb to the North Downs through Knockholt and eastbound out of Whitstable. In the non-electrified areas, 'track permits' were obtainable and proved invaluable for locations such as Herne Bay bank and the Minster triangle. One of the greatest challenges for a railway photographer in those days was to get an acceptable shot of the 'Night Ferry': it had to be the 'Up' train which arrived in London at about 9.00 a.m. because the 'Down' train ran in the dark. The 'Up' train was always difficult to photograph coming out of the rising sun as it approached the London suburbs but where else could one regularly see a Bulleid 'Light Pacific' double-headed by an L1 4–4–0?

The Modernization Plan of 1955 included two phases of Kent coast electrification and work was well under way by the end of 1957. Phase I embraced the ex-LC&DR lines from Gillingham to Ramsgate and Faversham to Dover plus the Sheerness branch. Major earthworks included quadrupling the running lines from Petts Wood Junction to Swanley Junction and from Gillingham to Newington; realignment of junctions at Shortlands and the complex intersection of the LC&DR and SER routes near Chislehurst. All this was done while the steam trains continued to run; steam finally ended on the Phase I lines in June 1959. Steam remained on most of the ex-SER lines but by 1960 diesels were starting to appear on both freight and secondary passenger services. Phase II of the Kent coast electrification covered the lines from Sevenoaks to Tonbridge, Ashford, Folkestone and Dover plus the secondary routes from Maidstone East to Ashford, Maidstone West to Paddock Wood, Ashford to Ramsgate via Canterbury West and Dover to Ramsgate via Deal and Minster. When this work was completed in June 1961 the steam era in Kent was finished except for the Allhallows and Grain services which remained steam operated until the end of 1961. The last steam train to run over the main lines in Kent was the LCGB 'Kentish Venturer' railtour on 25 February 1962.

Martin Galley
1990

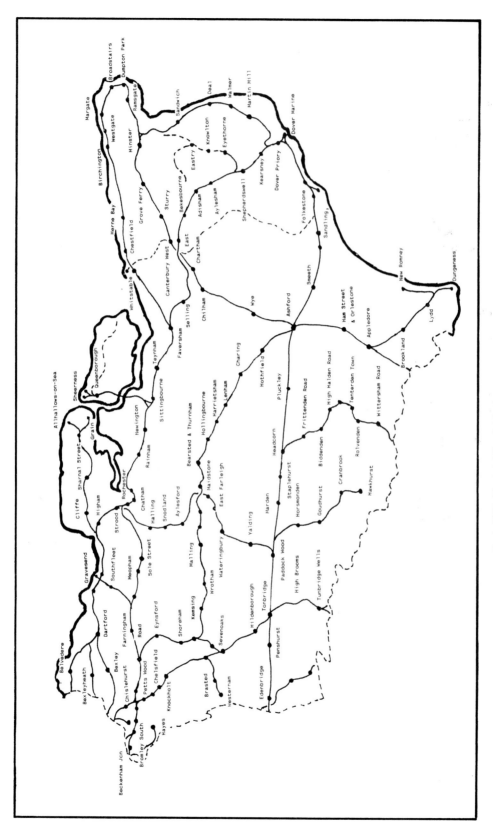

LAST DAYS OF STEAM IN KENT

(Only locations relevant to the text are shown)

The Chatham Line

'Schools' class No. 30923 *Bradfield*, in lined black livery, heads for Victoria through Beckenham Junction with the spur to the Mid-Kent line at New Beckenham diverging to the right.

March 1953

C class 0–6–0 No. 31579 storms past Beckenham Junction with a freight off the Mid-Kent line.
March 1953

Shunting the yard at Beckenham Junction on a Saturday evening is C class 0–6–0 No. 31293.
April 1953

With the 14.35 p.m. from Victoria to Dover via Chatham, 'Schools' class 4–4–0 No. 30920 *Rugby* heads for Bromley South from Shortlands.

17.8.53

Secondary passenger duties on the Kent coast main line were frequently entrusted to Maunsell 3-cylinder 'moguls'. In the late evening U1 No. 31901 drifts along from Bromley South to Shortlands with a train for Victoria.

14.8.53

L1 class 4–4–0 No. 31784 drifts down from Bromley South towards Shortlands with an 'Up' Ramsgate line train on a Monday evening. It was uncommon to see an L1 on the regular interval service trains, but No. 31784 was probably substituting for a failure or working back to Bricklayers Arms after the weekend excursion traffic.

17.8.53

'King Arthur' class 4–6–0 No. 30768 *Sir Balin* coasts into Bromley South with a train from Ramsgate to Victoria, while a venerable 4-SUB leads an Orpington train in the other direction.

25.5.53

When the Bulleid 'Pacifics' were temporarily withdrawn, several B1 4–6–0s helped out on Victoria to Ramsgate services. Here No. 61273 is leaving Bromley South for the Kent coast.

22.5.53

A Ramsgate to Victoria train coasts towards the stop at Bromley South behind 'King Arthur' 4–6–0 No. 30772 *Sir Percivale*.

March 1953

Helping out as in the previous photograph, here No. 61188 is leaving Bromley South for the Kent coast.

22.5.53

With the sun low in the sky 'Battle of Britain' 'Pacific' No. 34068 *Kenley*, with two Pullman cars towards the end of the train, heads a Victoria to Ramsgate express between Bickley and St Mary Cray Junctions.

28.11.53

An ugly but effective Q1 0–6–0 No. 33016, heading a freight from Hither Green to Dover via Maidstone East, is overtaken by 'Battle of Britain' 'Pacific' No. 34089 *602 Squadron* on a Victoria to Ramsgate train. This was before the days of quadruple track all the way to Swanley so the freight is being held on the connecting spur from Chislehurst, just short of St Mary Cray Junction.

22.12.53

N class 2–6–0 No. 31826 heads a freight from Hither Green for the Chatham line along the spur from Chislehurst towards St Mary Cray Junction.

22.12.53

'King Arthur' class 4–6–0 No. 30798 *Sir Hectimere* brings the 6.15 p.m. businessmen's train from Cannon Street to the Kent coast over the Chislehurst loop towards St Mary Cray Junction.

13.8.54

With a parcels train from the Chatham line, 3-cylinder N1 class 2–6–0 No. 31879 takes the spur to Chislehurst from St Mary Cray Junction.

7.7.57

With a small tender, 'King Arthur' class 4–6–0 No. 30794 *Sir Ector de Maris* wheels a Ramsgate train through St Mary Cray Junction.

April 1957

'Schools' class 4–4–0 No. 30915 *Brighton* rounds the curve from St Mary Cray Junction with an express for the Kent coast.

August 1954

With a freight from Hither Green that has just used the connecting spur from Chislehurst Junction to St Mary Cray Junction, N class 2–6–0 No. 31824 heads for Swanley and the Chatham main line.

September 1953

This section just east of St Mary Cray Junction is now widened to four tracks but when the picture was taken the footpath crossing near Hazelmere Road was a good spot for photography. An unidentified 'King Arthur' takes the all-Pullman 'Kentish Belle' to the coast.

September 1953

Taken before the line was widened to four tracks, a Chatham line freight train approaches Swanley Junction behind C class 0–6–0 No. 31575. The location is the footbridge just west of the present A20(T) bridge.

September 1953

Climbing towards the summit at Sole Street, U1 class 2–6–0 No. 31904 heads a Sunday morning Ramsgate train between Fawkham and Meopham.

14.7.57

At the same location, 'Schools' class 4–4–0 No. 30915 *Brighton* heads a similar train.

14.7.57

Going well on the climb to the summit at Sole Street, D1 class 4–4–0 No. 31545 heads a Sunday morning Ramsgate train near the site of the siding that once served the refuse disposal area between Fawkham and Meopham.

14.7.57

Climbing towards the summit at Sole Street, U1 class 2–6–0 No. 31909 heads a Sunday morning Ramsgate train.

14.7.57

Nearing the summit at Sole Street, N class 2–6–0 No. 31860 heads a Sunday morning excursion train to Ramsgate.

4.8.57

In the late Saturday evening sunshine U1 class 2–6–0 No. 31897 hurries through Chestfield on its way back to London with a train from Ramsgate.

9.8.58

Under the bridge at Ham Shades Lane, 'King Arthur' class 4–6–0 No. 30766 *Sir Geraint* heads for Chestfield with a Victoria to Ramsgate train.

27.7.58

An unidentified U1 class 2–6–0 tackles Sole Street bank with a returning excursion from the Kent coast on a Sunday evening.

25.8.57

A view from the train window as rebuilt 'West Country' 'Pacific' No. 34013 *Okehampton* threads across the viaducts west of Rochester before starting the ascent of Sole Street bank.

21.9.58

The water crane would not be required much longer as 'Schools' class 4–4–0 No. 30909 *St Paul's* arrives at Sittingbourne with a Ramsgate to Victoria train.

7.4.59

Through the apple orchards near Teynham, an unidentified U1 class 2–6–0 heads for Victoria with a train from Ramsgate.

30.8.58

In full flight for the Kent coast on a Sunday morning, E1 class 4–4–0 No. 31067 rounds a curve on the climb from Teynham towards Faversham.

17.8.58

With all the excursion traffic going the other way, E1 class 4-4-0 No. 31497 with its distinctive chimney, heads a westbound Sunday morning vans train towards Teynham.

17.8.58

A BR type 2 Bo-Bo diesel electric locomotive appears on a freight from Hither Green just a few days before electrification. Photographed between Teynham and Faversham there seems to be no shortage of footplate staff.

4.6.59

L class 4–4–0 No. 31768 drifts down towards Faversham with a local train that may have come from the Sheerness branch.

16.8.58

'King Arthur' class 4–6–0 No. 30795 *Sir Dinadan* climbs between Faversham and Teynham with a train for Victoria.

19.7.58

With its days on this line numbered, a rather shabby 'King Arthur' class 4–6–0 No. 30802 *Sir Durnore* struggles up the 1 in 132 from Faversham towards Teynham with a Ramsgate to Victoria train.

4.6.59

With a Saturday extra from Ramsgate, U1 class 2–6–0 No. 31895 tackles the climb from Faversham towards Teynham.

16.8.58

N class 2–6–0 No. 31414 pauses in Faversham station with a train of empty coal wagons, probably on their way to Snowdown colliery on the Dover line.

22.9.58

BR 'Standard' class 5 4–6–0 No. 73084 stops under the signal gantry at the country end of Faversham station. In the background is a well preserved birdcage brake end and Shepherd Neame's distinctive brewery.

22.9.58

Faversham shed yard with D1 class 4–4–0 No. 31509 in the foreground and BR 'Standard' class 2 2–6–2T No. 84029 behind, along with a collection of 'moguls' and C class 0–6–0s. Note the conductor rail already in position on the line to Whitstable which was energized in the spring of 1959.

27.12.57

In the late evening sunshine, an unidentified 'King Arthur' class 4–6–0 brings a Victoria train into Faversham from the Whitstable direction. On the left is part of Faversham yard and a small breakdown train, probably in use in connection with electrification work. A C class 0–6–0 stands in one of the shed roads on the right.

13.9.58

With a headcode suggesting a future passage of the Chislehurst loop towards London Bridge, rebuilt 'West Country' 'Pacific' No. 34013 *Okehampton* approaches the bridge at Graveney with a train from Whitstable.

30.8.58

'Schools' class 4–4–0 No. 30922 *Marlborough* accelerates under the bridge at Graveney to cross the marshes towards Whitstable with a Ramsgate train.

30.8.58

'Battle of Britain' class 'Pacific' No. 34067 *Tangmere* slows its Victoria to Ramsgate express from the sprint across the marsh at Seasalter in readiness for the stop at Whitstable. In the background can be seen beach huts along the sea wall behind the West Beach golf course.

29.3.59

Near the golf course at West Beach, Whitstable, E1 class 4–4–0 No. 31497 heads a vans train towards Faversham.

29.3.59

In the spring sunshine, 'Battle of Britain' class 'Pacific' No. 34086 *219 Squadron* accelerates away from Whitstable with a train for Victoria.

28.3.59

An unidentified D1 class 4–4–0 starts away up the steep climb from Whitstable station towards Herne Bay. This photograph was taken in the evening from the bridge that carried the Canterbury and Whitstable branch over the LC&DR main line.

1.8.58

E1 class 4–4–0 No. 31507 at Graveney, between Faversham and Whitstable, with a Sunday excursion to the Kent coast that had come via Nunhead and Chislehurst.

17.8.58

On a frosty day in December 1957, U1 class 2–6–0 No. 31893 crests the bank out of Whitstable station with a freight heading in the Ramsgate direction.

16.12.57

Laying down a smokescreen as it breasts the bank out of Whitstable station, 'Battle of Britain' 'Pacific' No. 34078 *222 Squadron* heads for Ramsgate with a train from Victoria.

3.8.58

Trailing a birdcage set and some vans, E1 4–4–0 No. 31506 nears Whitstable with a local for Faversham on a frosty morning.

16.12.57

With a well scorched smokebox door, 'Schools' class 4-4-0 No. 30938 *St Olave's* comes over the summit of Herne Bay bank on a Sunday morning excursion from Victoria to Ramsgate.

10.8.58

The all-Pullman, but anonymous, 'Kentish Belle' climbs away from Herne Bay behind rebuilt 'West Country' 'Pacific' No. 34005 *Barnstaple*.

3.8.58

Near the top of Herne Bay bank at Blacksole Lane bridge, U1 class 2–6–0 No. 31890, the erstwhile 3-cylinder 'River' class 2–6–4T, heads for Ramsgate with a Sunday excursion.

10.8.58

'King Arthur' class 4–6–0 No. 30802 *Sir Durnore* comes under Blacksole Lane bridge as it nears the top of Herne Bay bank with a Sunday excursion to Ramsgate.

10.8.58

Over the top of Herne Bay bank comes 'King Arthur' class 4–6–0 No. 30768 *Sir Balin* with a Sunday morning train for Ramsgate.

10.8.58

By the summer of 1958, BR 'Standard' class 5 4–6–0 locomotives had become regular performers on the Kent coast services. Here No. 73083 brings the Ramsgate bound 'Kentish Belle' over the summit of Herne Bay bank, showing the sharp change in gradient and the arches of Blacksole Lane bridge in the background.

10.8.58

With a clear exhaust, L class 4–4–0 No. 31767 nears the top of Herne Bay bank with an 'Up' train from the Kent coast.

10.8.58

The gradient post at the top of Herne Bay bank shows the rise of 1 in 100 from Herne Bay station changing to a descent of 1 in 115 towards the marshes near Reculver. The conductor rail is already in place for electrification in 1959.

10.8.58

BR 'Standard' class 5 4–6–0 No. 73086 starts away from Birchington with a train for Victoria. Newly laid conductor rail and new fencing is evidence of the changes which were to come a year later.

7.4.58

The gates are closed at the busy level crossing at Westgate for D1 4–4–0 No. 31145 to leave with its return excursion train destined for the North Kent line.

24.8.58

N class 2–6–0 No. 31412 takes its excursion train from London through the outskirts of Margate on its way to Broadstairs and Ramsgate.

24.8.58

Rebuilt 'West Country' 'Pacific' No. 34027 *Taw Valley* coasts down towards Margate with a train from Dover.

24.8.58

Heading back towards London, N class 2–6–0 No. 31400 approaches Margate from the Broadstairs direction.

24.8.58

'King Arthur' class 4–6–0 No. 30800 *Sir Meleaus de Lile* enters Ramsgate station with an excursion train that has come via the North Kent line, while rebuilt 'West Country' 'Pacific' No. 34012 *Launceston* marshals stock in the carriage sidings.

14.9.58

A Ramsgate bound steam train pauses at the island platform of Dumpton Park station.

14.9.58

There is close supervision of D1 class 4–4–0 No. 31739 being uncoupled from its train after arrival at Ramsgate station.

14.9.58

Preparing to depart for Deal, Dover and Charing Cross, 'Schools' class 4–4–0 No. 30937 *Clifton* stands in Ramsgate station.

14.9.58

A general view of Ramsgate's railway facilities, with the motive power depot on the left, carriage shed in the centre and station to the right. Although steam is much in evidence, so is the third rail ready for the electrification due to take place the following year.

14.9.58

The last D class in steam in Kent, but it is not about to go anywhere. No. 31501 is in use to provide steam for the carriage maintenance facilities at Ramsgate.

30.3.59

The Tonbridge Line

Q1 class 0–6–0 No. 33040 emerges from Chislehurst tunnel at Elmstead Woods station with a freight for the Tonbridge line.

30.10.60

'Battle of Britain' 'Pacific' No. 34075 *264 Squadron* heads a Charing Cross to Folkestone line train between Hither Green and Grove Park.

July 1953

L1 4–4–0 No. 31758 brings a special hop pickers' train of non-corridor stock into Chislehurst station on the 'slow' line, destined for the Weald of Kent.

22.9.56

Past the upper quadrant signals at the London end of Chislehurst station, an unidentified 'Schools' class 4–4–0 heads the 'Man of Kent' towards the coast.

22.9.56

With a birdcage set and a string of vans, 'King Arthur' class 4–6–0 No. 30804 *Sir Cador of Cornwall* is southbound through Petts Wood Junction. In the background the S-bend of one of the Chislehurst loops that connected Bickley with Petts Wood can be seen and in the foreground is the arc of the reverse connection.

August 1954

With a clear road at Petts Wood Junction, 'Battle of Britain' 'Pacific' No. 34076 *41 Squadron* heads
for Tonbridge with a train for Folkestone and beyond.

August 1954

An unidentified 'Schools' 4–4–0 on the London bound 'Man of Kent', with red and cream liveried
stock, passes the modern signalbox at Petts Wood Junction.

3.11.53

Passengers are waiting on the platform at Sevenoaks as 'Schools' class 4–4–0 No. 30920 *Rugby* arrives with a train for the Hastings line.

29.3.57

Carrying a headcode for Brighton via Eridge, C class 0–6–0 No. 31585 heads east with a freight through the centre road at Tonbridge station.

29.3.57

'Schools' class 4–4–0 No. 30910 *Merchant Taylors* pulls empty Hastings line stock out of the carriage sidings to the west of Tonbridge station.

16.7.55

A local train for Tunbridge Wells, headed by push–pull fitted H class 0–4–4T No. 31517, attacks the bank out of Tonbridge station.

15.4.57

Two years after its introduction had displaced the 'Schools' class, Hastings line class 6L diesel unit No. 1035 leaves Somerhill tunnel between Tonbridge and High Brooms.

10.4.59

About to leave Kent, 'Schools' class 4–4–0 No. 30930 *Radley* leaves Tunbridge Wells with a Hastings line train which has been lengthened by the addition of two non-corridor coaches. This service through Kent was to be the first to lose steam traction in the post-war era when the unique Hastings 'dmus' arrived in 1957.

29.12.56

C class 0–6–0 No. 31588 pilots a 'Schools' class 4–4–0 on a Hastings line train up the gradient from Tonbridge towards Tunbridge Wells.

15.4.57

'Schools' class 4–4–0 No. 30931 *King's Wimbledon* stands by the platform at Ashford with a mixed train for Canterbury West and Ramsgate.

5.7.60

The W class 2–6–4Ts spent most of their time in the London area with only occasional forays beyond Hither Green into Kent. Here, No. 31920 is immobilized in Ashford shed.

5.7.60

On the occasion of the RCTS 'Invicta' railtour, E and D class 4-4-0s Nos. 31166 and 31737 stand in the yard at Ashford MPD.

12.9.54

With Ashford Works in the background, 'West Country' 'Pacific' No. 34101 *Hartland* takes a boat train towards the Channel ports.

5.7.60

With steam to spare, an unidentified Bullied 'Light Pacific', on a Dover line train passes hop gardens near Paddock Wood.

15.9.56

At Folkestone Warren, 'Schools' class 4–4–0 No. 30936 *Cranleigh* bursts from Martello tunnel with a train for Dover.

3.9.54

On the Ashford to Folkestone section, 'Battle of Britain' 'Pacific, No. 34086 *219 Squadron* heads a 'Down' boat train near Sellindge between Smeeth and Westenhanger.

21.9.59

'Fairburn' 2–6–4T No. 42076 arrives at Minster station from the Ramsgate direction with a train of non-corridor stock, probably for the benefit of miners working at Chislet Colliery.

22.12.58

With a train for Deal and Ramsgate, rebuilt 'West Country' 'Pacific' No. 34003 *Plymouth* climbs out of Guston tunnel towards Martin Mill.

23.9.59

A view of Minster station from the footbridge looking west. A miners' train for Chislet Colliery and Ashford is departing from the platform.

22.12.58

Minster station, looking towards Canterbury.

22.12.58

'King Arthur' class 4–6–0 No. 30805 *Sir Constantine* heads an Ashford to Dover freight train around the west curve at Minster from the station towards the south junction.

22.12.58

'Fairburn' 2–6–4T No. 42076 approaches Minster station via the west curve with a train from Deal.
22.12.58

With an Ashford to Dover train, BR 'Standard' class 2 2–6–2T No. 84021 rounds the curve from Minster station to the South Junction.

22.12.58

With Minster station in the background, N class 2–6–0 No. 31402 heads a local train towards Ramsgate.

22.12.58

With a train from Margate to Ashford via Canterbury West, D1 class 4–4–0 No. 31739 arrives at Minster East Junction. The Minster avoiding line to Deal and Dover curves to the right.

22.12.54

L class 4–4–0 No. 31771 negotiates the curve between Minster station and Minster South Junction with a local train for Deal and Dover.

22.12.58

With Minster station in the background, 'Fairburn' 2–6–4T No. 42079 heads a local train towards Ramsgate.

22.12.58

With a train from Ramsgate to Ashford via Canterbury West, L class 4–4–0 No. 31780 arrives at Minster East Junction. The Minster avoiding line to Deal and Dover curves to the right.

22.12.58

With a Christmas mail train, D1 4–4–0 No. 31739 uses the Minster avoiding line and passes the east junction on its way from Deal to Ramsgate.

22.12.58

Boat Trains

One of the two 'Britannia' class 'Pacifics' allocated to Stewarts Lane in 1953, No. 70004 *William Shakespeare*, brings the Victoria bound 'Golden Arrow' through Beckenham Junction. Instead of the large arrows carried by the Bulleid 'Pacifics', smaller side arrows had to be made to fit the 'Britannia's' smoke deflectors.

May 1953

One of the Southern Railway designed 1-Co-Co-1 diesel electric locomotives No. 10202 heads the 'Golden Arrow' through Beckenham Junction on its way to Dover. Only provided with a headboard and no side arrows, this locomotive did not remain for long on the lines through Kent. The 'Golden Arrow' was to remain steam-hauled for another seven years before finally succumbing to electric locomotive haulage.

9.2.54

L1 class 4-4-0 No. 31754 pilots 'West Country' class 'Pacific' No 34102 *Lapford* on the Victoria bound 'Night Ferry' through Beckenham Junction. This was the usual motive power combination for this train for many years, the heavy load being only marginally within the capacity of an unassisted 'Merchant Navy'.

6.4.55

The temporary withdrawal of Bulleid 'Pacifics' in April and May 1953 because of the axle failure at Crewkerne resulted in the loan of locomotives from other regions. Here 'Britannia' class No. 70030 *William Wordsworth* brings the 'Night Ferry' from Dover past Shortlands Junction. Bulleid 'Light Pacifics' were usually given a pilot for this train but none was provided on this occasion.

22.5.53

Unrebuilt 'Merchant Navy' class No. 35030 *Elder Dempster Lines*, in blue livery, climbs past Downs Bridge, Shortlands, with a 'Down' boat train.

March 1953

The all-Pullman 'Golden Arrow' is hauled past Downs Bridge, Shortlands, by 'Battle of Britain' class 'Light Pacific' No. 34071 *601 Squadron.*

March 1953

Long before being rebuilt, and still in blue livery, 'Merchant Navy' class 'Pacific' No. 35028 *Clan Line* accelerates through Shortlands station with a 'Down' boat train.

17.8.53

With a young admirer perched on the footbridge wall, 'Britannia' 'Pacific' No. 70004 *William Shakespeare* passes the waterworks near Shortlands station with a boat train for the Tonbridge line.

22.8.53

An 'Up' boat train behind 'West Country' 'Pacific' No. 34103 *Calstock* coasts down from Bromley South to Shortlands and is passed by a semi-fast to Gillingham and Maidstone made up of 2-HAL units.

17.6.57

Boat trains had to be fitted in with the extensive excursion traffic on a summer Sunday morning. 'Merchant Navy' 'Pacific' No. 35028 *Clan Line* passes through Bromley South and would be routed via Tonbridge to Folkestone or Dover.

23.6.57

'Battle of Britain' 'Pacific' No. 34071 *601 Squadron* approaches Bickley station with an extra boat train from Victoria.

21.7.57

Passing 4-SUB emu No. 4341 in the carriage sidings, 'Battle of Britain' 'Pacific' No. 34072 *257 Squadron* approaches Bickley station with an extra boat train from Victoria.

21.7.57

Threading through the sharp curves of the connection between Chatham and Tonbridge lines, 'Battle of Britain' 'Pacific' No. 34072 *257 Squadron* eases a 'Down' boat train through Petts Wood Junction. About seven years from the time of this photograph, these curves had been realigned as part of the Kent coast electrification work.

November 1954

With an 'Up' boat train from Dover, routed via Chatham, 'Schools' class 4–4–0 No. 30900 *Eton* climbs towards Canterbury near Bekesbourne.

15.4.58

Unrebuilt 'Merchant Navy' class 'Pacific' No. 35028 *Clan Line* coasts into Tonbridge with a 'Down' boat train.

17.8.53

A stranger to the eastern section, rebuilt 'Merchant Navy' 'Pacific' No. 35015 *Rotterdam Lloyd* brings a heavy boat train from Dover up the gradient from Faversham towards Teynham, a duty that would soon be performed by electric locomotives and multiple units.

4.6.59

A pair of R1 class 0–6–0Ts Nos. 31069 and 31340, the former with a cut down cab, a relic of Canterbury and Whitstable branch operation, drift down the Folkestone harbour branch to be ready to assist another train up the bank.

20.4.58

By September 1959, the R1 class 0–6–0s had been replaced on the Folkestone harbour branch by ex-GWR '5700' class 0–6–0s. Here, Nos. 4692 and 4861 cross the harbour with a train for the junction.

21.9.59

Excursion Traffic

'King Arthur' class 4–6–0 No. 30794 *Sir Ector de Maris* pulls away from Bromley South with a Ramsgate train.

23.6.57

After waiting in the 'Down' siding for several trains to pass, D1 class 4–4–0 No. 31749 backed its train into the slow line platform at Bromley South to pick up passengers and sets off for the Kent coast.

23.6.57

Scraping the barrel for motive power on a busy summer Sunday as Maunsell Q class 0–6–0 No. 30540, carrying a Dover via Chatham headcode, leaves Bromley South with an excursion train.

23.6.57

Passing 4-SUB emu No. 4341 in the carriage sidings, Maunsell Q class 0–6–0 No. 30540 approaches Bickley station with a Sunday excursion train for Ramsgate.

21.7.57

A Sunday morning Ramsgate excursion, headed by E1 4–4–0 No. 31067, roars past St Mary Cray Junction on its way to the coast.

30.6.57

A Ramsgate excursion approaches St Mary Cray Junction behind an unidentified U1 2–6–0. The far track is the connecting spur from Chislehurst that was used by freights and businessmen's trains from Cannon Street.

7.7.57

With a Saturday evening train from Ramsgate to Victoria, U1 2–6–0 No. 31907 speeds down the gradient from Farningham Road to Swanley

6.7.57

There was a shortage of main line motive power on a busy summer Sunday as an unidentified Maunsell Q class 0–6–0, carrying a Dover via Chatham headcode, approaches St Mary Cray Junction with an excursion train.

7.7.57

With a Saturday evening train from Dover to Victoria, E1 4–4–0 No. 31504 speeds down the gradient from Farningham Road to Swanley.

6.7.57

Struggling through a rain shower on the climb to the summit at Sole Street, C class 0–6–0 No. 31267 heads a Sunday morning excursion to Ramsgate made up of ex-GWR stock between Fawkham and Meopham.

14.7.57

With a local train from the Dover line, L1 class 4–4–0 No. 31755 climbs from Faversham towards Teynham

16.8.58

'Schools' class 4–4–0 No. 30908 *Westminster* pulls away from Whitstable with a London train.

3.8.58

Along the straight from Chestfield towards Whitstable, 'Black 5' 4–6–0 No. 45404 brings an excursion train of ex-LMS stock back towards London after a Sunday at the Kent coast.

27.7.58

Under the bridge at Ham Shades Lane, 'King Arthur' class 4–6–0 No. 30793 *Sir Ontzlake* heads for Chestfield with a Victoria to Ramsgate train.

27.7.58

On a summer Sunday morning L1 class 4–4–0 No. 31783 starts the attack of Herne Bay bank as it pulls away from the station with an excursion train. The leading coach is an old 'continental' brake end followed by non-corridor stock.

3.8.58

With a London bound train, L1 class 4–4–0 No. 31786 passes through Herne Bay station as a 'Down' train stops in the station and another train for London, headed by a 'mogul', waits in the loop platform.

2.8.58

It was unusual to see 'Fairburn' 2–6–4Ts on the Kent coast main line but here No. 42098 descends Herne Bay bank on a Sunday morning, probably with an empty stock working for the London area.

3.8.58

An excursion from the Midland Region, made up of ex-LMS stock, makes a clean start up Herne Bay bank behind 'Black 5' 4–6–0 No. 45310.

3.8.58

With a lot of smoke, U1 class 2–6–0 No. 31904 tackles Herne Bay bank on an excursion train for Ramsgate that has probably come via the Catford loop line.

3.8.58

A signal failure at the top of Herne Bay bank causes N class 2–6–0 No. 31811 to be given the green flag as it heads for Reculver with a Sunday excursion to Ramsgate.

20.7.58

Unusual motive power for the Kent coast main line, BR 'Standard' class 4 4–6–0 No. 75068 climbs Herne Bay bank with an excursion for Ramsgate.

10.8.58

The E1 class 4–4–0 with the odd chimney, No. 31497, nears the top of Herne Bay bank with a Kent coast excursion train from the Nunhead line and Chislehurst loop.

10.8.58

The Secondary and Branch Lines

Ex-LC&DR R class 0–4–4T No. 31671 stands at Sheerness-on-Sea station while working the RCTS
'Invicta' railtour. This tour took in the whole of the Kent coast.

12.9.54

An unidentified D1 class 4–4–0 prepares to depart tender first from Sheerness-on-Sea with the branch train for Sittingbourne.

7.4.59

The RCTS 'London and North Kent' railtour visited Gravesend West at the end of the branch from Farningham Road, which had lost its passenger service in 1953 and was about to be attenuated. E1 class 4–4–0 No. 31507 had brought in the ex-LNER stock.

21.3.59

Sheerness Dockyard station in use for carriage sidings. There appeared to be no intention of electrifying this backwater.

7.4.59

An early post-war experiment with railbuses was this 3-car ACV dmu, which was tested on the Gravesend to Allhallows-on-Sea branch in October and November 1953. Seen here at Allhallows-on-Sea, the rough riding train of 4-wheel cars awaits another trip.

2.11.53

Q1 class 0–6–0 No. 33036 stands with an Allhallows branch push–pull set in the centre road at Gravesend Central.

25.9.60

H class 0–4–4T No. 31512, with a special 3-coach train for the 'Railway Enthusiasts' Club', takes water in the centre road at Gravesend Central.

25.9.60

With the end of steam operation in sight, H class 0–4–4T No. 31530 departs from Sharnal Street with the Allhallows branch train.

2.12.61

H class 0–4–4T No. 31530 propels the Allhallows branch train near Cliffe across the Hundred of Hoo, by now one of the last surviving steam operations in Kent.

8.7.61

The presence of several photographers is evidence that the end of steam operation is near as H class 0–4–4T No. 31324 departs from Sharnal Street for Gravesend with the Allhallows branch train.

2.12.61

At Sharnal Street on the Allhallows branch from Gravesend, N class 2–6–0 No. 31815 pauses with a freight train on its way towards Grain. Sharnal Street was a junction for the Kingsnorth Light Railway and the Chattenden Naval Tramway.

4.6.54

In the wintry sunlight, H class 0–4–4T No. 31530 departs from Allhallows-on-Sea with the branch train for Gravesend.

2.12.61

The inspectors confer as H class 0–4–4T No. 31512 stands at Allhallows-on-Sea with the 'Railway Enthusiasts Club' special.

25.9.60

The old and the new crossed at Canterbury where U1 class 2–6–0 No. 31900 on a Ramsgate to Ashford train passes under the electrified Faversham to Dover line. It was at this exact point that the Elham Valley line once diverged to Folkestone.

18.8.60

A few minutes after the previous photograph was taken, an all-electric Dover to Victoria boat train passed on the ex-LC&DR line, led by two motor luggage vans.

18.8.60

'Fairburn' class 2–6–4T No. 42098 passes Grove Ferry with a Ramsgate to Ashford train, via Canterbury West.

19.9.59

With an Ashford to Maidstone East train, N class 2–6–0 No. 31407 approaches Charing station. Some signalling alterations appear to be in progress.

10.9.60

On the Maidstone East to Ashford line, a BR standard class 2 2–6–2T coasts tender first into Charing with a local for Ashford.

10.9.60

H class 0–4–4T No. 31512 was piloted by BR 350 hp diesel shunter No. D3721 when the 'Railway Enthusiasts Club' special visited Chatham dockyard.

25.9.60

H class 0–4–4T No. 31530 passes the signalbox and water tower at Westerham as it takes the branch train back to Dunton Green.

29.10.55

The Westerham branch train with H class 0–4–4T No. 31322 passing an empty goods yard as it nears its terminus.

4.10.59

Although located in Kent, Tunbridge Wells West mostly served the ex-LB&SCR routes into Sussex and Surrey. Here C class 0–6–0 No. 31716 arrives with a freight from the Eastbourne line, while C2X No. 32529 simmers in the shed yard behind.

10.1.57

An Oxted line train from Victoria has finished its journey at Tunbridge Wells West behind 'Fairburn' 2–6–4T No. 42103, while a push–pull train waits alongside.

10.1.57

Just in Kent, near Edenbridge, a Redhill to Tonbridge train hauled by an unidentified L class 4-4-0 crosses over the Oxted to Ashurst line, which is partially in tunnel at this location.

14.8.54

H class 0-4-4T No. 31533 trundles along with the Westerham branch train near Brasted.

15.4.61

D1 class 4–4–0 No. 31505 arrives at Bekesbourne with the local train for Dover.

26.3.59

A typical LC&DR line station at Selling on the line between Canterbury and Dover.

23.3.59

A local service from Ashford to Dover, via Minster and Deal, leaves Walmer behind 'Fairburn' 2–6–4T No. 42077.

30.7.56

By the summer of 1960, steam was being gradually replaced on the ex-SER lines in Kent. A brand new BR type 3 Bo-Bo diesel electric No. D6515 heads a Dover to Ramsgate train near Walmer.

21.7.60

The conductor rail was already laid as H class 0–4–4T No. 31324 heads a Paddock Wood to Maidstone West train alongside the River Medway near Wateringbury.

22.4.61

With a train from Maidstone West to Tonbridge, H class 0–4–4T No. 31544 pulls a birdcage set out of the platform and onto the main line at Paddock Wood.

9.4.56

There are no holiday-makers around as BR standard class 4 2–6–4T No. 80041 waits in the rain at New Romney with the branch train for Appledore.

5.7.60

With the train too long for the platform at Hawkhurst, passengers on the RCTS 'Wealden Limited' railtour detrain onto the track. H class 0–4–4T No. 31177 had brought the train in from Paddock Wood.

14.8.55

Freight services on the southern section of the K&ESR lingered on. New Year's Day, 1958, and A1X class 0–6–0T No. 32636 departs from Northiam with a train for Tenterden.

1.1.58

On the last day of passenger operation on the K&ESR, A1X 0–6–0T No. 32655 waits to leave Rolvenden for the final sharp climb to Tenterden at the end of its journey from Robertsbridge. The larger than normal passenger load had overflowed to the leading birdcage end. The 'Terriers' were to survive on the K&ESR for a few more years to operate a freight service on the southern section.

2.1.54

After shunting the yard at Tenterden, A1X class 0–6–0T No. 32636 stands ready to take its train back to Robertsbridge.

1.1.58

With the closure notice posted and only a few more days of operation to go on the northern section of the K&ESR, O1 class 0–6–0 No. 31065 waits to leave High Halden Road with a train from Headcorn to Tenterden.

29.12.53

In the last summer of steam operation on the K&ESR, O1 0–6–0 No. 31064 coasts down the bank from Tenterden and into Rolvenden with a short train from Headcorn.

19.8.53

It was always difficult to photograph trains on the ex-LC&DR line into Dover because of the north–south orientation and the deep cuttings. Here, L1 4-4-0 No. 31753, with a birdcage set, emerges from Lydden tunnel with a train for Dover.

31.8.54

Within the recently electrified confines of Dover Priory station, a veteran O1 class 0-6-0 No. 31370 waits for its next duty. These locomotives were retained for a while to work the stub end of the EKR from Shepherdswell to Eythorne Colliery.

23.9.59

C class 0–6–0 No. 31112 with a freight train at Dover harbour.

31.12.60

Although the East Kent Railway beyond Eythorne Colliery ceased to operate in 1951, the track remained in place for several years until the summer of 1954 when it was removed. O1 class 0–6–0 No. 31258 heads the track lifting train at the site of Knowlton Halt.

31.8.54

Kent Coast Electrification

Oops! N class 2–6–0 No. 31810 has run out of track in the midst of the alterations to layout taking place at Shortlands. The hoarding on the right advertised the Kent Coast Electrification to come in 1959.

13.4.58

A veteran 4-SUB No. 4516 on a Victoria to Orpington service uses the loop from Bickley to Petts Wood Junction. In the background can be seen the realigned spurs provided to ease speed restrictions at this point.

1.1.59

N class 2–6–0 No. 31823 brings a freight train for the Chatham line over the spur from Chislehurst and past the track alterations at St Mary Cray Junction.

1.1.59

'King Arthur' class 4–6–0 No. 30803 *Sir Harry le Fise Lake* slowly passes the reconstruction work at St Mary Cray Junction with a train from Dover to Victoria via Chatham. The newly laid tracks to St Mary Cray can be seen beyond the signalbox, but they are not yet connected.

1.1.59

'King Arthur' class 4–6–0 No. 30769 *Sir Balan* heads a Victoria to Ramsgate train towards St Mary Cray Junction. In contrast to earlier photographs at this location, the widening to four tracks has been completed and new crossovers provided.

1.1.59

In the midst of trackwork alterations for the Kent coast electrification, U1 class 2–6–0 No. 31907 passes the old signalbox at Newington with a Ramsgate to Victoria train.

6.7.58

Surrounded by trackwork alterations for the Kent coast electrification, 'Battle of Britain' class 'Pacific' No. 34082 *615 Squadron* passes the old signalbox at Newington with a boat train from Dover to Victoria.

6.7.58

The inaugural electric train, the 'Kent Coast Special', led by 4-BEP unit No. 7005 departs from Whitstable station on its way to Ramsgate on Tuesday 9.6.59. Full electric service did not start until Monday 15.6.59 so steam survived for a further five days.

9.6.59

Relegated to vans train duties, BR standard class 5 4–6–0 No. 73041 heads for Faversham at West Beach, Whitstable.

5.6.59

Driver training for the forthcoming electric trains was provided by two push–pull trailers marshalled at either end of H class 0–4–4T No. 31308, seen here at Bekesbourne station.

26.3.59

Practising for the big day, 2-EPB No. 5604 is used for driver training and passes West Beach, Whitstable, en route to Faversham.

5.6.59

With the current switched on already, BR electric locomotive No. E5004 was tried out with an empty stock working at West Beach, Whitstable.

5.6.59

An unidentified Bulleid 'Light Pacific' brings a 'Down' boat train past the new electric traction depot at Chart Leacon near Ashford.

28.5.61

Diesel traction was becoming commonplace on the Ashford to Ramsgate via Canterbury line in the summer of 1960. BR type 3 Bo-Bo No. D6515 nears Canterbury at a point close to the site of the junction with the former Elham Valley line. This view is now marred by the presence of the new A2(T) bypass around Canterbury.

27.8.60

The End of Steam in Kent

A once proud 'Schools' class 4–4–0 No. 30921 *Shrewsbury* is relegated to cable-train duties and is seen here passing the ugly brick signalbox at Petts Wood Junction.

15.4.61

While the colour light signalling receives some attention, 'Schools' class 4–4–0 No. 30937 *Epsom* arrives at Faversham station with a Ramsgate train.

6.6.59

A surprisingly clean 'Schools' class 4–4–0 No. 30938 *St Olave's* runs through Faversham station with an extra for Ramsgate.

6.6.59

In the aftermath of the cessation of steam operation on the Chatham line, Faversham MPD yard reflected the new order. A solitary C class 0–6–0 No. 31715 stands with a BR type 2 diesel and a 350 hp shunter while an emu enters the carriage sidings.

22.6.59

'Schools' class 4–4–0 No. 30909 *St Paul's* runs through Faversham station with an extra for Ramsgate.

6.6.59

A sad occasion, but there was still to be steam on the Dover line for a couple of years. 'Schools' class 4–4–0 No. 30925 *Cheltenham* stands on the turntable at Ramsgate MPD on the last day of steam operation on the Chatham line.

14.6.59

On the last day of steam operation over the Kent coast lines, 'Schools' class 4–4–0 No. 30910 *Merchant Taylors* stands in Ramsgate station after arrival from Victoria.

14.6.59

C class 0–6–0 No. 31255 stands outside Faversham shed during the last week of steam operation on the Kent coast lines.

6.6.59

On the last day of steam operation over the Kent coast lines, 'Schools' class 4–4–0 No. 30938 *St Olave's* passes the West Beach golf course near Whitstable with an excursion train for Ramsgate.
14.6.59

Even on the last day of steam operation, a foreign locomotive appeared at Ramsgate on an excursion train from the Midland Region. A 'Black 5' class 4–6–0 is being turned, while a new electric unit waits in the background to assume its duties the next day.

14.6.59

In the evening of the last day of steam operation on the Chatham line, the driver of 'Schools' class 4–4–0 No. 30915 *Brighton* lubricates the motion while awaiting departure to Victoria from Ramsgate. The colour light signals do not look as if they will be ready for the big day.

14.6.59

Steam-hauled boat trains were still in evidence when this picture was taken on the ex-LC&DR line as 'West Country' class 'Pacific' No. 34101 *Hartland* heads through Bromley South with the 9.30 a.m. boat train from Victoria, which was carrying a headcode for the Chatham line to Dover. This extraordinary routing for a steam working in 1961 must have been due to a problem or electrification work on the ex-SER route through Tonbridge and Ashford.

4.2.61

Old habits die hard as BR type 2 Bo-Bo diesel No. D5012 takes water in Ramsgate station.

31.12.60

The scene on the last day of steam operation over the ex-LC&DR Kent coast lines, at the eastern end of Ramsgate MPD. Two 'King Arthur' class and two 'Schools' class stand ready to take return service trains and excursions back to London via the Chatham route for the last time.

14.6.59

The Pullman cars in the 'Golden Arrow' have been joined by more mundane stock as rebuilt 'West Country' 'Pacific' No. 34100 *Appledore* hauls the 'Down' train up the gradient from Beckenham Junction to Shortlands, the day before the end of scheduled main line steam in Kent.

10.6.61

Steam-hauled boat trains were still in evidence on the ex-LC&DR line as late as March 1961 as rebuilt 'Battle of Britain' class 'Pacific' No. 34077 *603 Squadron* traverses the new 4-track section between St Mary Cray and Swanley carrying a headcode for the Chatham line to Dover.

4.3.61

In contrast to some earlier photographs, rebuilt 'Battle of Britain' class 'Pacific' No. 34089 *602 Squadron* heads a 'Down' boat train along the new connecting spur from Bickley to Petts Wood Junction.

4.3.61

As the LCGB 'Kentish Venturer' railtour progressed around the coast, the weather deteriorated rapidly and by the time 'King Arthur' class 4–6–0 No. 30782 *Sir Brian* reached Martin Mill it was snowing hard. A cold and dreary end for the last day of steam in Kent.

25.2.62

The last main line steam train in Kent was the LCGB 'Kentish Venturer' railtour, which made a clockwise tour of the Kent coast. It is seen here breasting the summit of Herne Bay bank behind 'King Arthur' class 4–6–0 No. 30782 *Sir Brian*.

25.2.62